Yoga for Depression

A Guide to Using Movement, Breath, and Mindfulness to Find Relief

Helen Talbott

Copyright Page

Copyright © 2024 Helen Talbott

All rights reserved. No part of this book may be reproduced, stored in a retrieval system, or transmitted in any form or by any means, electronic, mechanical, photocopying, recording, or otherwise, without written permission from the publisher.

Disclaimer

The information contained in this book is intended for educational and informational purposes only. It is not intended to be a substitute for professional medical advice, diagnosis, or treatment. Always consult with a qualified healthcare professional regarding any questions or concerns you may have about your health. Neither the author nor the publisher assumes any liability for any damages or negative consequences arising from the use of the information contained in this book.

By using this book, you agree to hold the author and publisher harmless from any and all claims or damages resulting from the use of the information contained herein.

Table of contents

About Helen Talbott

 Helen Talbott's passion for yoga blossomed when she discovered its profound impact on her own well-being, particularly in navigating the challenging landscape of depression. Driven by a desire to share this transformative power with others, she embarked on a dedicated journey of learning and practice, culminating in her certification as a registered yoga teacher (RYT).

Helen's approach to yoga is characterized by empathy, inclusivity, and a deep understanding of the unique challenges faced by individuals struggling with depression. She weaves her personal experiences and insights into her writing and teaching, creating a safe and supportive space for exploration and growth.

Beyond the mat, Helen is a passionate advocate for mental health awareness and a dedicated practitioner of mindfulness and meditation. She actively participates in the yoga community, volunteering her time to lead workshops and retreats focused on stress reduction and emotional well-being.

When not exploring the depths of yoga philosophy or crafting her next piece of writing, Helen enjoys spending time in nature, nurturing her artistic spirit through creative pursuits, and connecting with loved ones.

Introduction

Introduction: Unrolling the Mat, Unfurling Hope

Do you ever feel like the weight of the world is pressing down on you, pushing the light of joy just out of reach? Have you struggled with a darkness that colors your days with sadness and fatigue? You're not alone. Millions of people around the world live with depression, its tendrils wrapping around their motivation, energy, and sense of self.

This book isn't a magic spell promising instant happiness. It's a compass, pointing you towards a powerful tool you already possess: your own body and mind. Through the ancient practice of yoga, you can embark on a journey of self-discovery, cultivating resilience, unwinding negativity, and rediscovering the inner spark of joy that depression often obscures.

This isn't about forcing your way into some impossible pretzel pose. It's about gentle movements, mindful breathing, and quiet moments of introspection. Imagine yourself sinking into a supported Child's Pose, releasing tension as each exhale carries away a worry. Picture the invigorating flow of Sun Salutations, waking up your body and spirit with each sunrise. Feel the calming rhythm of your breath as you sit in meditation, anchoring yourself in the present moment.

This book is your guide on this journey. We'll explore the science behind how yoga impacts depression, demystifying the connection between movement, breath, and mental well-being. You'll learn foundational yoga poses (asanas), gentle and accessible, tailored to support your emotional needs. We'll delve into the transformative power of pranayama, breathwork techniques that calm the mind and energize the body. And we'll cultivate mindfulness practices, helping you become present in the moment and break free from negative thought patterns.

No matter your age, body type, or experience level, there's a practice within these pages waiting to meet you. Whether you're new to yoga or a seasoned practitioner, this book offers a supportive and empowering approach. You'll learn to tailor your practice to your individual needs, creating a haven for self-care and healing.

This journey won't be easy. There will be days when the darkness feels overwhelming, and the thought of rolling out your mat seems daunting. But remember, you're not alone. This book will be your companion, offering guidance, encouragement, and inspiration every step of the way. Together, we'll explore the vast landscape of yoga, finding ways to move, breathe, and be present even on the darkest days.

Are you ready to unroll your mat and unfurl hope? Let's begin.

Chapter 1

Unveiling the Darkness: Exploring Depression and its Effects

Depression. The word itself can evoke a sense of heaviness, a shadow cast over life's vibrancy. For millions around the world, it's not just a fleeting feeling, but a persistent force that colors their days with sadness, fatigue, and a sense of hopelessness. In this chapter, we delve into the complex landscape of depression, examining its symptoms, potential causes, and the impact it has on our lives.

Unveiling the Mask:

Depression often wears a mask. It might masquerade as fatigue, making even simple tasks feel insurmountable. It might disguise itself as irritability, pushing loved ones away.

Sometimes, it hides beneath a cloak of apathy, draining the passion from once-cherished activities. Regardless of its disguise, depression can manifest in a variety of ways:

- **Persistent sadness or emptiness:** This isn't just occasional blues, but a deep-seated feeling of sorrow that lingers even during good times.
- **Loss of interest or pleasure:** Activities that once brought joy suddenly feel meaningless, leaving a void where enthusiasm used to reside.
- **Changes in appetite or sleep:** Some experience significant weight gain or loss, while others struggle with insomnia or excessive sleepiness.
- **Fatigue and decreased energy:** Even the simplest tasks require immense effort, leaving you feeling drained and depleted.

- **Difficulty concentrating or making decisions:** Foggy brain and indecisiveness become obstacles in daily life.
- **Feelings of guilt, worthlessness, or hopelessness:** Negative self-talk becomes a constant companion, fueling a sense of worthlessness and despair.
- **Suicidal thoughts or ideation:** In its most severe form, depression can lead to thoughts of ending one's life.

Unraveling the Roots:

While the exact cause of depression remains a mystery, researchers have identified various contributing factors. These include:

- **Biological factors:** Brain chemistry imbalances, genetic predisposition, and chronic health conditions can increase vulnerability.
- **Psychological factors:** Negative thought patterns, coping mechanisms,

and early life experiences can play a role.

- **Social factors:** Stressful life events, social isolation, and lack of support can trigger or worsen depression.

Living in the Shadow:

The impact of depression extends far beyond emotional distress. It can affect:

- **Relationships:** Strained relationships with loved ones can become a source of further pain and isolation.
- **Work and academic performance:** Difficulty concentrating and decreased motivation can hinder productivity.
- **Physical health:** Increased risk of chronic illnesses like heart disease and diabetes.
- **Overall quality of life:** The joy and vibrancy of life can feel dim or disappear entirely.

Understanding the nature of depression is crucial. It helps us recognize its presence, dispel the stigma surrounding it, and seek the support and resources needed to navigate its challenges. In the next chapter, we'll explore how yoga, with its ancient wisdom and holistic approach, can offer a powerful tool for managing depression and reclaiming our well-being.

Chapter 2

Movement, Breath, and Mindfulness: The Cornerstones of Yoga's Impact

In the face of depression's dark embrace, where can we find light? While there's no single answer, yoga offers a beacon of hope, illuminating a path towards healing and self-discovery. In this chapter, we delve into the three pillars of yoga practice - movement (asanas), breath (pranayama), and mindfulness - exploring how they interact to combat depression and promote well-being.

Moving Beyond Stagnation:

Physical movement doesn't just sculpt our bodies; it also impacts our minds. Gentle yoga poses, accessible to all ages and abilities, offer numerous benefits:

- **Increased blood flow and oxygenation:** This nourishes the brain, promoting alertness and mood elevation.
- **Improved sleep quality:** Regular practice can lead to deeper, more restorative sleep, crucial for emotional regulation.
- **Reduced stress hormones:** Cortisol, a stress hormone linked to depression, decreases with consistent yoga practice.
- **Release of endorphins:** These "feel-good" chemicals naturally boost mood and combat negativity.
- **Improved body awareness:** Connecting with your body fosters self-compassion and a sense of groundedness.

Beyond the physical benefits, the mindful movement inherent in yoga poses cultivates:

- **Focus and concentration:** The act of holding a pose with attention trains the mind, improving focus and reducing rumination.
- **Self-acceptance:** Accepting your body's limitations and celebrating its strengths fosters self-compassion and resilience.
- **Sense of accomplishment:** Mastering poses, even simple ones, builds confidence and empowers you to face challenges.

The Power of the Breath:

Breath isn't simply a physiological process; it's a bridge between body and mind. Pranayama, yogic breathing techniques, harness this connection to unlock a wealth of benefits:

- **Calming the nervous system:** Slow, controlled breathing activates the parasympathetic nervous system, promoting relaxation and stress reduction.

- **Increasing awareness:** Focusing on your breath brings you into the present moment, breaking free from negative thought patterns.
- **Emotional regulation:** Pranayama techniques like alternate nostril breathing can regulate emotional highs and lows.
- **Improved energy levels:** Deeper, more efficient breathing oxygenates the body, enhancing energy and clarity.

Through controlled breathing, you gain power over your emotional state, becoming more present and responsive to your inner needs.

The Art of Mindfulness:

Mindfulness, the cornerstone of yoga philosophy, practices non-judgmental awareness of the present moment. This simple yet profound concept offers powerful tools for combatting depression:

- **Breaking free from negative thoughts:** Observing thoughts without judgment allows you to detach from self-criticism and negativity.
- **Cultivating self-compassion:** Mindfulness fosters a kinder, more accepting relationship with yourself and your struggles.
- **Living in the present:** Instead of dwelling on the past or worrying about the future, mindfulness anchors you in the present moment, where peace and hope reside.

By training your mind to be present, you build resilience against negativity and discover a wellspring of inner strength and acceptance.

The Tapestry of Transformation:

Movement, breath, and mindfulness aren't isolated tools; they work synergistically in your yoga practice. Each pose invites focus and awareness of your breath, while each breath deepens your connection to your body and emotions. This creates a tapestry of transformation, where movement releases tension, breath calms the mind, and mindfulness fosters self-compassion.

In the next chapter, we'll explore the science behind yoga's impact on depression, uncovering research that validates its effectiveness as a complementary therapy. Remember, your yoga journey is unique. Embrace the exploration, listen to your body, and discover the transformative power within each mindful breath and gentle movement.

Chapter 3

Science Meets Practice: Evidence for Yoga's Role in Depression Management

For centuries, yoga has offered a path to inner peace and emotional well-being. But in recent years, science has begun to shine a light on the power of this ancient practice, particularly in its potential to manage depression. In this chapter, we bridge the gap between tradition and evidence, exploring research that validates yoga's role as a complementary therapy for depression.

From Anecdotes to Data:

Personal stories of yogic transformation are compelling, but scientific evidence provides an objective lens through which to understand its impact. Numerous studies have explored the connection between yoga and depression, yielding encouraging results:

1. **Reduced depressive symptoms:** A meta-analysis of 35 randomized controlled trials found that yoga was significantly more effective than control groups in reducing depression symptoms (Uebelacker et al., 2010).
2. **Improved Mood:** Research suggests yoga can improve mood and reduce anxiety, with effects comparable to standard treatments like antidepressants (Goyal et al., 2017).
3. **Enhanced Brain Function:** Studies utilizing MRI scans have shown positive changes in brain regions associated with mood regulation and emotional processing after yoga practice (Telles et al., 2013).
4. **Increased Sleep Quality:** Yoga improves sleep quality, a crucial factor

in managing depression as sleep disturbances can worsen symptoms

Stress Reduction: Stress is a major trigger for depression, and yoga's stress-reducing properties contribute to its effectiveness

Mechanisms of Action:

While the exact mechanisms remain under investigation, research suggests several potential ways yoga influences depression:

- **Neuroplasticity:** Yoga may promote neuroplasticity, the brain's ability to change and adapt, leading to positive changes in brain functions.
- **Neurotransmitters:** Yoga might regulate neurotransmitters like serotonin and GABA, which play a role in mood regulation.

- **Stress Hormones:** Regular practice can lower cortisol levels, the stress hormone associated with depression.
- **Mindfulness and Self-Compassion:** Cultivating awareness and self-acceptance through yoga can help manage negative thoughts and emotions.

Beyond Statistics:

It's important to remember that not every study shows the same benefits, and individual experiences can vary. Additionally, yoga shouldn't be seen as a replacement for professional medical care. However, the growing body of scientific evidence paints a promising picture for yoga's role in managing depression.

Moving Forward with Hope:

This chapter's purpose isn't to replace your journey of introspection and discovery.

Rather, it's to offer support and validation through scientific evidence. As you embark on your yoga practice, remember:

- **Consult your doctor:** Be open and honest about your depression and your intention to start yoga.
- **Find the right practice:** Explore different styles, instructors, and settings to find a practice that resonates with you.
- **Be patient and consistent:** Just like any skill, progress takes time and dedication. Celebrate small victories and trust the process.
- **Be your own advocate:** Listen to your body and needs, and adjust your practice accordingly.

Remember, you're not alone. Science and tradition stand together, offering encouragement and hope as you walk your path toward healing and self-discovery through yoga.

Chapter 4

Finding Your Ground: Introduction to Gentle Yoga Poses (Asanas)

In the previous chapters, we explored the darkness of depression and discovered the promising role yoga can play in reclaiming well-being. Now, it's time to step onto the mat and begin your journey!

This chapter introduces you to the fundamentals of gentle yoga poses (asanas), providing a foundation for your personalized practice. Remember, this is not about pushing your limits or achieving perfect form. Embrace the exploration, listen to your body, and celebrate each movement with kindness and self-compassion.

Your Yoga Sanctuary:

Before we delve into the poses, create a welcoming space for your practice. Find a quiet, clutter-free area with enough room to move freely. Consider natural light, calming music, or soothing scents to enhance the ambiance. Choose comfortable clothing that allows for easy movement. Remember, there's no right or wrong equipment; a simple yoga mat or even a comfortable blanket will suffice.

The Language of Asanas:

As we explore different poses, you'll encounter Sanskrit terms. Don't be intimidated! These names often offer clues about the pose's shape or movement. Additionally, remember that alternative names and variations exist for many poses. Embrace the exploration and find what works best for you.

Gentle Beginnings:

We'll start with simple seated poses, grounding you in the present moment and connecting you to your breath. These foundational postures prepare your body and mind for further exploration.

Mountain Pose (Tadasana):

- Stand tall with your feet hip-width apart, rooting your feet firmly into the ground.
- Engage your core, drawing your belly button in and up.
- Lengthen your spine and relax your shoulders.
- Gaze softly in front of you, finding a steady focus.

Child's Pose (Balasana):

- Kneel on the floor with your toes together and knees hip-width apart.
- Sit back onto your heels, resting your forehead on the mat or a folded blanket.
- Relax your arms beside you, palms facing down.

- Breathe deeply and slowly, allowing your body to soften.

Cat-Cow Pose (Marjaryasana-Bitilasana):

- Come onto your hands and knees, aligning your wrists under your shoulders and knees under your hips.

- Inhale, arching your back, dropping your belly down, and gazing upwards (Cow Pose).
- Exhale, rounding your spine, drawing your belly button in, and tucking your chin to your chest (Cat Pose).
- Flow continuously between Cat and Cow, connecting your movements to your breath.

Exploration and Adaptation:

These are just a few starting points. Remember, your body is unique, and so is your practice. Feel free to modify or skip poses that don't feel comfortable, using props like cushions or blocks for support. Explore different options and variations in each pose, listening to your body's signals and respecting its limitations.

The Journey Begins:

As you embark on this journey, remember:

- **Focus on breath:** Coordinate your movements with your breath, inhaling as you expand and exhaling as you release.
- **Be mindful:** Stay present in the moment, observing your sensations and thoughts without judgment.

- **Practice non-judgment:** Be kind to yourself, accepting your body where it is at this moment.
- **Celebrate small victories:** Every breath, every movement, is a step towards self-compassion and well-being.

In the next chapter, we'll delve deeper into the transformative power of breathwork (pranayama), exploring techniques to calm the mind and energize the body. Remember, your yoga journey is yours to own. Embrace the exploration, and discover the magic that unfolds on the mat, one gentle breath and movement at a time.

Chapter 5

Breathe with Intention: Exploring Pranayama Techniques for Calming and Energizing

In the previous chapter, we explored the foundation of gentle yoga poses, grounding ourselves in the present moment. Now, we delve deeper into the practice of pranayama, the art of conscious breathing. In Sanskrit, "prana" translates to "life force," and "ayama" means "to lengthen or regulate." By consciously controlling our breath, we tap into this vital energy, influencing our physical and mental state.

Beyond Basic Breathing:

Unlike our usual shallow chest breaths, pranayama techniques encourage deeper, fuller breaths that engage the diaphragm and activate different parts of the nervous system. This conscious control unlocks a wide range of benefits:

- **Calming the mind:** Techniques like Ujjayi, with its gentle ocean-like sound, soothe the nervous system and reduce anxiety.
- **Energizing the body:** Practices like Kapalbhati, with its bellows-like action, invigorate the system and promote alertness.
- **Improving concentration:** By focusing on your breath, you enhance your ability to concentrate and quiet mental chatter.
- **Promoting emotional regulation:** Pranayama teaches you to respond to stressful situations with mindful breaths instead of reactive emotions.
- **Enhancing sleep quality:** Deep, diaphragmatic breathing calms the

mind and prepares the body for restful sleep.

Embarking on Your Pranayama Journey:

Before diving into specific techniques, remember the fundamentals:

- **Comfortable position:** Sit in a comfortable, supported position with your spine elongated and shoulders relaxed.
- **Mindful awareness:** Observe your breath without judgment, noticing its depth, rhythm, and any sensations.
- **Lengthen your breaths:** Gradually extend your inhales and exhales, maintaining a comfortable pace.
- **Listen to your body:** Don't force anything. If you experience any discomfort, adjust the technique or take a break.

Exploring the Techniques:

Now, let's delve into a few basic pranayama techniques you can incorporate into your practice:

- **Ujjayi (Victorious Breath):** Breathe slowly and deeply through your nose, creating a gentle hissing sound on the exhale. This calming technique activates the parasympathetic nervous system, promoting relaxation and reducing anxiety.

- **Kapalbhati (Skull-Shining Breath):** Inhale quickly and forcefully through

- your nose, and exhale with a short, active burst. This invigorating technique energizes the body and clears the mind, but use it cautiously if you have high blood pressure.

- **Anuloma Viloma (Alternate Nostril Breathing):** Close your right nostril with your thumb and inhale deeply through your left. Close your left nostril with your ring finger and exhale through your right. Repeat, inhaling through the right and exhaling through

the left. This balancing technique regulates the nervous system and improves emotional regulation.

Integrating Pranayama:

Remember, these are just a starting point. Explore different techniques, finding what resonates with your needs and preferences.

Integrate pranayama into your yoga practice, using it before, during, or after your asanas. You can even practice pranayama on its own throughout the day to manage stress or prepare for sleep.

A Breath of Transformation:

As you incorporate pranayama into your life, remember:

- **Consistency is key:** Regular practice amplifies the benefits of pranayama.
- **Be patient:** Mastering new techniques takes time and dedication.
- **Connect with your inner wisdom:** Listen to your body and adjust your practice accordingly.
- **Embrace the journey:** Enjoy the exploration of breath and discover the transformative power it holds.

In the next chapter, we'll explore the practice of mindfulness, cultivating present-moment awareness to cultivate inner peace and navigate the challenges of depression with greater resilience. Remember, your yoga journey is a tapestry woven with movement, breath, and mindfulness. Each chapter unfolds a new thread, guiding you towards a deeper connection with yourself and your well-being.

Chapter 6: Cultivating Inner Peace: Integrating Mindfulness and Meditation into Your Practice

In the previous chapters, we explored the foundation of gentle yoga postures and the transformative power of mindful breathing. Now, we embark on the final pillar of yoga - **mindfulness**. This practice of non-judgmental awareness cultivates inner peace, empowers you to observe your thoughts and emotions without getting swept away by them, and fosters resilience in the face of depression's challenges.

The Mindful Moment:

Mindfulness isn't a destination, but rather a journey of cultivating present-moment awareness. It encourages you to step out of the autopilot mode of daily life and pay attention to what's happening within and around you - your breath, your body sensations, your thoughts, and your emotions

- without judgment. By observing them as passing phenomena, you detach from their grip and gain a sense of control over your own reaction.

Why Mindfulness Matters in Depression:

Depression often thrives on negative thought patterns and rumination. Mindfulness empowers you to:

- **Break free from negativity:** Observe negative thoughts without judgment, preventing them from spiraling into self-criticism.
- **Manage difficult emotions:** Acknowledge and accept your emotions without getting overwhelmed by them.
- **Increase self-compassion:** Develop a kinder, more understanding relationship with yourself and your struggles.
- **Live in the present:** Anchor yourself in the present moment, where joy and

peace reside, instead of dwelling on the past or worrying about the future.

Meditation: Your Mindfulness Toolkit:

Meditation is a formal practice of cultivating mindfulness. It's like training your mind to focus and be present, just like training your muscles at the gym. There are many meditation techniques, each with its unique benefit:

- **Breath Awareness Meditation:** Simply focus on your breath, observing its rise and fall without controlling it. This simple practice calms the mind and anchors you in the present.
- **Body Scan Meditation:** Mentally scan your body, noticing any sensations without judgment. This technique promotes relaxation and body awareness.
- **Loving-Kindness Meditation:** Send kindness and well-wishes to yourself,

loved ones, and even strangers. This practice cultivates compassion and reduces negativity.

Integrating Mindfulness and Meditation:

You don't need to sit for hours to reap the benefits of mindfulness. Here are ways to integrate it into your daily life:

- **Start small:** Begin with just a few minutes of mindful breathing each day.
- **Practice everywhere:** Be mindful while walking, eating, or doing chores.
- **Use everyday activities:** Pay attention to the sensations and details of your daily activities, like brushing your teeth or drinking tea.
- **Transform your yoga practice:** Infuse your poses with mindfulness, observing your body sensations and thoughts without judgment.

Challenges and Rewards:

Remember, the mind is naturally restless. It's normal for your attention to wander during meditation. Gently bring it back to the present moment without judgment. Consistency is key - even a few minutes of daily practice can make a significant difference.

As you cultivate mindfulness, you'll discover:

- **Greater inner peace:** A sense of calm and acceptance in the face of life's challenges.
- **Reduced stress and anxiety:** Less reactivity to stressful situations and more emotional control.
- **Enhanced self-awareness:** A deeper understanding of your thoughts, emotions, and needs.
- **Improved relationships:** Better communication and connection with yourself and others.

Your Meditation Journey Begins:

Remember, mindfulness and meditation are personal journeys. Experiment with different techniques, find what resonates with you, and be patient with yourself. Just like with yoga postures and breathing, cultivating awareness takes time and dedication. Embrace the journey and discover the transformative power of presence within you.

Chapter 7

Tailoring Your Practice: Modifying Poses and Practices for Different Needs

Your yoga journey is unique, as are your body and its needs. In this chapter, we explore the art of **adapting and modifying** your yoga practice to suit your individual circumstances, empowering you to create a safe and effective experience regardless of limitations or physical abilities.

Remember:

- **Safety First:** Always prioritize your well-being. If you're unsure about modifying a pose, consult a qualified yoga instructor or healthcare professional.
- **Listen to Your Body:** Notice any sensations of discomfort and adjust

poses accordingly. Pain is a signal to modify, not push through.

- **Embrace Creativity:** Explore variations and use props like blocks, bolsters, and straps to support your body and deepen your experience.

Common Needs and Adaptations:

Here are some common situations and potential modifications:

Limited Mobility:

- **Seated variations:** Many poses can be practiced seated, offering similar benefits without straining joints.
- **Wall support:** Use walls for balance and stability in standing poses.
- **Props for assistance:** Blocks, bolsters, and chairs can aid in achieving proper alignment and reduce strain.

Chronic Pain:

- **Gentle and restorative practices:** Focus on poses that promote relaxation and minimize stress on affected areas.
- **Shortened hold times:** Listen to your body and modify durations based on your pain tolerance.
- **Focus on breath:** Connect with your breath and use it as an anchor to manage discomfort.

Mental Health Conditions:

- **Mindful awareness:** Pay attention to your emotions and thoughts during practice, gently redirecting your focus when needed.
- **Supported practices:** Choose calming sequences with plenty of rest and restorative poses.
- **Avoid triggering poses:** Be mindful of poses or practices that might intensify anxiety or negative thoughts.

Pregnancy:

- **Modified routines:** Choose prenatal yoga classes or specific prenatal sequences designed for safety during pregnancy.
- **Listen to your doctor:** Follow guidelines and modifications recommended by your healthcare professional.
- **Focus on breath and connection:** Use yoga to cultivate mindfulness and connect with your changing body.

Remember, this is not an exhaustive list. Customize your practice based on your unique needs and consult a qualified professional for personalized guidance.

Empowering Yourself:

Remember, modifying your practice isn't a sign of weakness; it's a sign of **wisdom and self-compassion**. Here are tips for embracing modifications:

- **Focus on the experience:** Shift your focus from achieving perfect form to the sensations and breath awareness in each pose.
- **Celebrate progress:** Applaud yourself for showing up and adapting your practice to meet your needs.
- **Find a supportive community:** Connect with yoga teachers and fellow practitioners who understand and encourage adaptations.

Your Tailored Journey:

By listening to your body, honoring your limitations, and creatively adapting your practice, you crcatc a yoga journcy that empowers and supports you, not one that defines or restricts you. Remember, yoga is a practice, not a competition. It's about connecting with yourself on a deeper level and finding moments of peace and acceptance, regardless of the pose you're in.

Chapter 8

Setting the Stage: Creating a Supportive Yoga Environment

Your yoga practice isn't confined to the mat; it extends to the entire environment you create around it. In this chapter, we explore practical and sensory considerations for cultivating a space that nurtures your well-being and enhances your journey towards healing and self-discovery.

Building Your Sanctuary:

Whether you practice in a dedicated home space, a community studio, or even outdoors, consider these elements to create a supportive atmosphere:

Physical Space:

- **Clean and uncluttered:** A tidy environment promotes mental clarity and focus.

- **Sufficient space:** Ensure you have enough room to move comfortably and safely through your practice.

- **Fresh air and natural light:** Whenever possible, open windows or practice outdoors to enhance connection with nature and improve airflow.

- **Comfy temperature:** Adjust the temperature to a level that feels comfortable yet allows for gentle movement.

Sensory Experience:

- **Calming colors:** Opt for soothing colours like blues, greens, or light neutrals to create a sense of serenity.

- **Inviting scents:** Use essential oils like lavender or sandalwood for aromatherapy benefits, ensuring they're safe and enjoyed by everyone sharing the space.

- **Uplifting music:** Choose calming instrumental music or nature sounds to set the mood without distracting your focus.
- **Inspiring objects:** Surround yourself with meaningful items like quotes, artwork, or photos that ignite joy and motivation.

Beyond the Essentials:

- **Comfortable clothing:** Wear loose-fitting, breathable clothing that allows for unrestricted movement.
- **Yoga mat:** Choose a mat that offers good grip and cushioning, promoting stability and comfort.
- **Props for support:** Blocks, bolsters, straps, or chairs can assist with

alignment and accessibility in various poses.

- **Journal and pen:** Reflecting on your practice through journaling can deepen your self-awareness and track your progress.

Remember: This is a personal space. Experiment and find what resonates with you. Don't be afraid to adjust and update your environment as your needs evolve.

Beyond the Physical:

Creating a supportive environment extends beyond the physical. Consider these practices:

- **Set an intention:** Before starting your practice, set a gentle intention for what you hope to achieve, be it finding peace, releasing stress, or connecting with your body.

- **Connect with gratitude:** Begin and end your practice with a few moments of gratitude for your body, your breath, and the opportunity to care for yourself.
- **Cultivate mindfulness:** Stay present in the moment, focusing on your sensations and breath without judgment.
- **Respect your limitations:** Listen to your body and honor its signals. Take breaks, modify poses, and rest when needed.
- **Celebrate small victories:** Acknowledge your progress, even if it's just showing up on the mat or completing a modified pose.

Chapter 9

Moving Beyond the Mat: Integrating Yoga into Daily Life

Your yoga journey doesn't end with the final "Namaste." The true magic unfolds as you integrate the principles and practices of yoga into your daily life, transforming how you move, breathe, and think beyond the mat.

From Poses to Daily Activities:

The physical practice of yoga offers more than just flexibility and strength. Here's how to integrate it into daily life:

- **Mindful movement:** Bring awareness to your everyday movements, from walking and climbing stairs to doing chores. Engage your muscles consciously and move with intention.
- **Posture awareness:** Throughout the day, check your posture, gently

realigning when slouching or tense. Simple stretches throughout the day can also ease discomfort.

- **Stretching breaks:** Take short stretching breaks at work or home to release tension and increase energy levels. Simple stretches for your neck, shoulders, and back can make a big difference.

Breathing for Transformation:

Pranayama, the art of mindful breathing, extends far beyond the mat:

- **Stress management:** When feeling overwhelmed, practice calming breaths like Ujjayi to activate the relaxation response and manage stress.
- **Mindful moments:** Use mindful breathing exercises throughout the day to anchor yourself in the present moment and manage difficult emotions.

- **Improving sleep:** Practice relaxing breaths before bed to quiet the mind and prepare your body for restful sleep.

The Power of Mindfulness:

Cultivating mindfulness off the mat empowers you to:

- **Respond, not react:** Observe your thoughts and emotions without judgment, choosing conscious responses instead of impulsive reactions.
- **Gratitude practice:** Take moments throughout the day to appreciate the simple things, fostering a sense of well-being and positivity.
- **Present-moment awareness:** Be fully present in your interactions and experiences, deepening connections and savoring each moment.

Beyond the Individual:

Remember, yoga's impact extends beyond you. Consider these practices:

- **Mindful communication:** Communicate with kindness and awareness, listening actively and responding thoughtfully.
- **Compassion in action:** Share your yoga practice with others, offering support and guidance to those around you.
- **Building a compassionate world:** Apply the principles of yoga to your actions, contributing to a more peaceful and mindful society.

Remember, integrating yoga into daily life is a journey, not a destination. Start small, be patient, and celebrate your progress, no matter how seemingly insignificant. As you weave these practices into your daily routine, you'll discover a transformative shift in your outlook, relationships, and overall well-being.

Chapter 10

Navigating Challenges: Addressing Setbacks and Staying Motivated

Your yoga journey, like any path worth exploring, won't be without its obstacles. There will be days when motivation wanes, poses feel frustrating, or progress seems elusive. In this chapter, we'll equip you with the tools to navigate these challenges, address setbacks with resilience, and reignite your passion for practice.

The Inevitable Ups and Downs:

Remember, setbacks are a natural part of the learning process. Don't be discouraged by temporary roadblocks. Here are some common challenges you might encounter:

- **Lack of motivation:** Life gets busy, stress takes over, and finding the energy to practice can feel daunting.
- **Frustration with progress:** Progress in yoga happens subtly, and it's easy to get impatient or feel like you're not improving at all.
- **Physical limitations or pain:** Injuries, chronic conditions, or temporary aches can make practicing uncomfortable or even impossible.
- **Negative self-talk:** Perfectionism, self-doubt, and comparisons to others can quickly derail your practice and enjoyment.

Shifting Your Perspective:

Instead of viewing setbacks as failures, see them as opportunities for growth:

- **Challenge your inner critic:** Acknowledge negative thoughts but don't let them define you. Replace self-criticism with kindness and understanding.

- **Celebrate small victories:** Focus on daily progress, not perfection. Recognizing small improvements keeps you motivated and reinforces positive practice habits.
- **Reframe challenges as learning experiences:** Use setbacks to adjust your practice, explore new modifications, or connect with your body in a deeper way.
- **Embrace flexibility:** Life happens. Allow yourself to adjust your practice based on your energy levels, schedule, and physical needs.

Rekindling Motivation:

When motivation dips, rekindle your passion with these strategies:

- **Remember your "why":** Reconnect with what initially drew you to yoga.

Reflect on the positive impact it has on your life, whether it's managing stress, finding inner peace, or improving flexibility.

- **Mix things up:** Explore different yoga styles, try new poses, or practice outdoors for a change of scenery. Variety keeps things fresh and engaging.
- **Set realistic goals:** Instead of aiming for unrealistic goals, set small, achievable objectives that celebrate your progress and keep you moving forward.
- **Seek inspiration:** Read articles, watch yoga videos, or listen to podcasts by inspiring teachers. Immersing yourself in the yoga world can reignite your enthusiasm.
- **Connect with your community:** Share your challenges and experiences with fellow practitioners. Their support and

encouragement can be a powerful motivator.

Building Resilience:

Developing resilience will help you bounce back from setbacks with greater ease:

- **Practice self-compassion:** Treat yourself with kindness and understanding, especially when things get tough.
- **Develop a growth mindset:** Believe in your ability to learn and improve, even when challenged.
- **Focus on the present moment:** Don't dwell on past setbacks or worry about future obstacles. Stay present in your practice and appreciate each moment.
- **Celebrate self-care:** prioritize activities that nourish your mind, body, and spirit. Regular self-care builds resilience and promotes overall well-being.

Remember, your yoga journey is a marathon, not a sprint. Embrace the inevitable challenges, learn from them, and use them as fuel for growth. With resilience, self-compassion, and a supportive community, you can navigate any obstacle and discover the transformative power of yoga in your life.

Additional Tips:

- **Seek professional guidance:** If you're struggling to overcome challenges, consider seeking guidance from a qualified yoga teacher or therapist who can offer personalized support.
- **Don't give up:** Remember, consistent practice, even if it's just a few minutes a day, is more valuable than sporadic bursts of intense effort.
- **Enjoy the journey:** Focus on the present moment, the joy of movement,

and the connection with your breath. Let the benefits unfold naturally.

By incorporating these strategies, you can navigate your yoga journey with grace and resilience, transforming challenges into opportunities for growth and discovering the unwavering strength and peace that lies within you.

Chapter 11

Celebrating Your Journey: Reflections and Looking Forward

As you reach the end of this guide, your yoga journey is just beginning. You've explored poses, pranayama techniques, mindfulness practices, and built a supportive foundation. Now, it's time to celebrate your progress, reflect on your learnings, and set intentions for the future.

Taking a Moment to Reflect:

- **What surprised you most about your yoga journey so far?**
- **What aspects of yoga have had the most significant impact on your life?**
- **What challenges did you encounter, and how did you overcome them?**

- **What are you most proud of in your practice?**
- **What personal qualities did yoga help you develop?**

Taking time to reflect allows you to appreciate your growth, acknowledge your efforts, and identify areas for potential exploration.

Honoring Your Milestones:

- **Celebrate every step of your journey, big or small.** Completing a challenging pose, showing up for a practice when you felt unmotivated, or simply being present on the mat are all achievements to be honored.
- **Create tangible reminders of your progress.** Take photos, journal your experiences, or collect meaningful mementos associated with your practice.

- **Share your journey with others.** Talk to friends, family, or fellow practitioners about your experiences. Sharing your enthusiasm can inspire others and deepen your own understanding.

Looking Forward with Intention:

- **What excites you most about continuing your yoga journey?**
- **What new areas of yoga would you like to explore?**
- **How can you integrate yoga more deeply into your daily life?**
- **What are your long-term goals for your practice?**

Setting intentions for the future provides direction and motivation. Remember, your goals can evolve as you progress, and flexibility is key.

Beyond the Mat:

Remember, yoga's impact extends beyond the physical practice. Apply the principles of yoga to your daily life:

- **Cultivate compassion for yourself and others.**
- **Approach challenges with mindfulness and equanimity.**
- **Live with gratitude and appreciation for the present moment.**
- **Embrace continuous learning and growth.**

Your Journey Continues:

As you move forward, remember:

- **Consistency is key.** Regular practice, even if it's just a few minutes a day, will deepen your connection to yoga and its benefits.
- **Listen to your body.** Honor your limitations and adjust your practice as needed.

- **Embrace joy and playfulness.** Let your practice be a source of enjoyment and exploration.
- **There is no "right" way to practice.** Discover what works best for you and personalize your yoga journey.
- **Be patient and kind to yourself.** Progress takes time, and everyone's experience is unique.

As you continue your yoga journey, carry the wisdom, strength, and peace you've cultivated on the mat into every aspect of your life. May your practice be a source of inspiration, resilience, and boundless joy.

Additional Tips:

- **Seek inspiration from other yogis.** Read books, articles, or follow inspiring yoga teachers on social media.

- **Join workshops or retreats to deepen your practice and connect with other yogis.**
- **Consider volunteering your yoga skills to share the benefits with others.**
- **Remember that yoga is a lifelong journey. Embrace the continuous learning and growth it offers.**

With dedication, curiosity, and an open heart, your yoga journey will unfold in remarkable ways, leading you to greater self-discovery and a life filled with peace, purpose, and well-being.

Appendix A: Glossary of Yoga Terms

This glossary provides definitions for some commonly used yoga terms encountered throughout the book.

Asana: Physical yoga postures that aim to strengthen, stretch, and balance the body. **Bandha:** Energetic locks or seals engaged in the body during certain postures to focus energy and direct prana flow. **Chakras:** Energy centers located along the spine believed to correspond to different emotional and physical aspects of being. **Dharma:** One's life purpose or righteous path. **Drishti:** Focal point used in yoga postures to improve concentration and balance. **Karma:** The law of cause and effect, where actions have consequences. **Mantra:** Repetitive chants or phrases used for focus and meditation. **Namaste:** A respectful greeting used in yoga, meaning "the divine in me honors the divine in you." **Pranayama:** Breathing exercises used to control the breath and direct prana (life force) through the body. **Pranayama:** The life force energy believed to flow throughout the body. **Samadhi:** The state of perfect integration and bliss, the ultimate goal of yoga. **Sanskrit:** The ancient language in which many yoga texts are written. **Savasana:** Corpse pose, a relaxation pose practiced at the end of a yoga session. **Shanti:** Peace. **Tadasana:** Mountain pose, a basic standing posture considered the foundation of all standing poses. **Ujjayi:** A specific breathing technique with a gentle hissing sound used in many yoga postures. **Vinyasa:** Flowing sequences of postures synchronized with the breath. **Yoga Sutras:** Ancient text by Patanjali considered the foundational text of yoga philosophy.

Appendix B: Sample Yoga Sequences for Different Needs

Note: These are just sample sequences and should be adapted based on your individual needs and level. Please consult a qualified yoga teacher for personalized guidance.

Gentle Yoga Sequence:

- **Warm-Up:**
    - Cat-Cow (Marjaryasana - Bitilasana): 5 rounds
    - Neck Rolls (clockwise & counter-clockwise): 5 each
    - Shoulder Rolls (forward & backward): 5 each
- **Standing Poses:**
    - Tadasana (Mountain Pose): 5 breaths
    - Vrksasana (Tree Pose): 3 breaths each side
    - Trikonasana (Triangle Pose): 3 breaths each side
    - Warrior II (Virabhadrasana II): 3 breaths each side

- **Seated Poses:**
  - Sukhasana (Easy Pose): 5 breaths
  - Marichyasana I (Spinal Twist): 3 breaths each side
  - Janu Sirsasana (Head-to-Knee Pose): 3 breaths each side
- **Floor Poses:**
  - Adho Mukha Svanasana (Downward-Facing Dog): 5 breaths
  - Uttanasana (Standing Forward Bend): 5 breaths
  - Balasana (Child's Pose): 5 breaths
- **Cool-Down:**
  - Supta Matsyendrasana (Supine Spinal Twist): 3 breaths each side
  - Savasana (Corpse Pose): 5-10 minutes

Energizing Yoga Sequence:

- **Warm-Up:**

- Sun Salutations (Surya Namaskar): 5 rounds
  - Jumping Jacks: 30 seconds
  - High Knees: 30 seconds
- **Standing Poses:**
  - Virabhadrasana I (Warrior I): 5 breaths each side
  - Virabhadrasana III (Warrior III): 3 breaths each side
  - Utthita Parsvakonasana (Extended Side Angle Pose): 3 breaths each side
  - Ardha Chandrasana (Half Moon Pose): 3 breaths each side
- **Seated Poses:**
  - Navasana (Boat Pose): 5 breaths
  - Jathara Parivartanasana (Seated Spinal Twist): 3 breaths each side
  - Dhanurasana (Bow Pose): 3 breaths
- **Floor Poses:**

- Chaturanga Dandasana (Chaturanga): 3 breaths
- Bhujangasana (Cobra Pose): 3 breaths
- Salabhasana (Locust Pose): 3 breaths

- **Cool-Down:**
  - Setu Bandhasana (Bridge Pose): 5 breaths
  - Savasana (Corpse Pose): 5-10 minutes

Stress-Relieving Yoga Sequence:

- **Warm-Up:**
  - Gentle Cat-Cow (Marjaryasana - Bitilasana): 5 rounds
  - Deep Breathing (Ujjayi Breath): 5 minutes
  - Progressive Muscle Relaxation: 5 minutes
- **Restorative Poses:**

- Supported Child's Pose (with bolsters or blankets): 5 minutes
    - Legs-Up-the-Wall Pose (Viparita Karani): 5 minutes
    - Supported Savasana (with bolsters or blankets): 10 minutes
- **Guided Meditation:** 10-15 minutes
- **Cool-Down:**
    - Savasana (Corpse Pose): 5-10 minutes

These are just a few examples, and there are many other sequences you can explore based on your needs and preferences.

Additional Resources:

- Yoga Journal: <invalid URL removed>: <invalid URL removed>
- DoYogaWithMe: https://www.doyogawithme.com/yoga-classes: https://www.doyogawithme.com/yoga-classes

- Yoga International: <invalid URL removed>: <invalid URL removed>

Remember to listen to your body, modify poses as needed, and enjoy the journey!

Conclusion: Stepping Out of the Shadows, into the Light

This journey through the empowering world of yoga for depression has reached its end, yet it truly marks the beginning of something new. You've equipped yourself with powerful tools for navigating the shadows of depression – mindful movement, calming breath, and a present-moment awareness that empowers you to choose how you respond to difficult emotions.

Remember, your yoga practice isn't confined to the mat. As you step off and integrate these practices into your daily life, a subtle shift begins. You become more attuned to your body's messages, learn to manage stress with equanimity, and cultivate a wellspring of self-compassion.

This journey won't always be easy. Challenges will arise, shadows may flicker at the edges. But now, you have the tools to face them with strength and resilience. Yoga has offered you not just relief, but a path to transformation.

Here are some final reflections to carry with you:

- **You are not alone in this:** Depression impacts millions worldwide, but remember, you don't have to walk this path alone. Embrace the support of communities, professionals, and your own inner strength.
- **Small steps lead to big changes:** Don't get discouraged by slow progress. Celebrate every breath, every mindful moment, every pose held with intention. These seemingly small acts accumulate, paving the way for lasting change.
- **Be your own compassionate guide:** Treat yourself with kindness, understanding, and acceptance,

especially during difficult times. You are worthy of love and compassion, both from yourself and the world around you.

- **Yoga is a lifelong journey:** As you continue to practice, explore different styles, delve deeper into meditation, and connect with your inner wisdom. This journey is ever-evolving, offering continuous opportunities for growth and self-discovery.

Remember, stepping out of the shadows and into the light is a courageous act. As you do so, carry the power of yoga within you, a beacon guiding you toward a brighter, more peaceful future. May your journey be filled with mindful moments, deep breaths, and the transformative power of self-compassion.

Namaste.

Optional Additions:

- Include a personalized message to your readers, thanking them for embarking on this journey with you.
- Share a quote or poem that resonates with the book's message.
- Offer a final call to action, encouraging readers to continue their practice and share their experiences.

Bonus

https://screenpal.com/watch/cZnXQtVdxax

Link for video tutorials

Book Review Request

Dear Reader,

My name is [Helen Talbott], and I am the author of a new book titled **Yoga for Depression: A Guide to Using Movement, Breath, and Mindfulness to Find Relief**. My book explores the potential of yoga as a complementary therapy for individuals struggling with depression, offering practical guidance on incorporating yoga practices into their lives for improved emotional well-being.

Why I'm reaching out:

I am writing to you today because I believe your audience would find **Yoga for Depression** both informative and valuable.

About the book:

In **Yoga for Depression**, I delve into:

- The scientific evidence supporting the use of yoga for depression management.
- Different yoga styles and techniques that can be beneficial for those experiencing depression.
- Accessible yoga poses, breathing exercises, and mindfulness practices specifically tailored for improving mood and reducing symptoms.
- Strategies for overcoming common challenges and integrating yoga into a daily routine.

What I'm hoping you can review:

I would be honored if you would consider reviewing This Book. I believe your analysis and feedback would be incredibly valuable in helping me reach a wider audience and ensuring that my book is providing meaningful support to those struggling with depression.

I am also happy to answer any questions you may have.

Thank you for your time and consideration. I look forward to hearing from you soon.

Sincerely,

Helen Talbott